ANXIETY DISORDER SOLUTIONS

SOLUTIONS

The Essential Guide to Overcoming Anxiety
and Panic Attacks

S.E. Charles

DEDICATION

This book is dedicated to those in search of essential information and practical skills to help manage and control anxiety and panic attacks.

CONTENTS

INTRODUCTION

Anxiety disorders can be really disabling and can interfere with your regular schedule of activities. They have the potential to impact undesirably on your relationships, studies or job performance.

When it comes to mental health issues, anxiety disorders are very common. Some experts describe them as the most common among mental disorders. They affect an estimated 3 of 10 adults at a point in their lives.

The lifetime rates of anxiety in the United States are, strangely, among the highest in the world. This was estimated at around 29 percent. Apart from substance use disorder, anxiety disorders make for the most common psychiatric complaint in America.

In this insightful guide, you will learn useful techniques, essential information and practical skills to help you manage and control your anxiety and panic attacks

CHAPTER 1 – OVERVIEW OF ANXIETY DISORDERS AND THEIR CAUSES

There is absolutely nothing unusual about anxiety. We all feel anxious for one reason or another at times. The feeling could result when getting ready to take a test or when preparing to make a vital decision.

Anxiety disorders are a different thing altogether, however. We discuss these conditions in this chapter, in which you will also learn about their possible causes.

What are Anxiety Disorders?

Anxiety is simply a feeling that arises due to anticipation of a future event, which gives rise to worry or fear. It tenses and puts you in a fight-or-flight mode. In other words, it makes you alert to situations and causes you to either tackle them headlong or avoid them altogether.

Under normal conditions, this feeling should be occasional and temporary.

Anxiety disorders, on the other hand, are nothing like "normal" anxiety. These are mental illnesses that make people become anxious and cause the feeling to linger, possibly getting worse over time.

Anxiety disorders can be really disabling and can interfere with your regular schedule of activities. They have the potential to impact undesirably on your relationships, studies or job performance.

The negative effects that these disorders may cause could make affected individuals to avoid known triggers. This means, for instance, that you may start avoiding your workplace if that's where the problem lies.

Before anybody can be said to suffer from an anxiety disorder, the fear or worry such experiences must be considered to be out of proportion, with relation to the trigger. Anxiety disorder may also be suspected if the level of anxiety is a bit too high for your age.

The feeling also needs to interfere with your ability to function normally in some way to be considered an anxiety disorder.

The different types of these mental illnesses include:

- Generalized anxiety disorder
- Panic disorder
- Agoraphobia
- Social anxiety disorder
- Separation anxiety disorder
- Specific phobias

These mental illnesses are not limited to certain age groups. They affect both adults and children. The symptoms they may produce include:

- Nervousness
- Shortness of breath
- Dry mouth
- Nausea
- Tense muscles
- Heart palpitations

How Common Are Anxiety Disorders?

When it comes to mental health issues, anxiety disorders are very common. Some experts describe them as the most common among mental disorders. They affect an estimated 3 of 10 adults at a point in their lives.

There were about 273 million cases around the world as of 2010, according to a systematic analysis for the Global Burden of Disease Study 2010.

The lifetime rates of anxiety in the United States are, strangely, among the highest in the world. This was estimated at around 29 percent by a source. Apart from substance use disorder, anxiety disorders make for the most common psychiatric complaint in America.

Women are more like to experience these illnesses than men.

What Causes Anxiety Disorders

The exact causes of these conditions are not yet fully known. But, as in the case of other mental illnesses, anxiety disorders are believed to be the result of a combination of factors. These include:

- Environmental factors
- Genetics
- Psychological Factors
- Physical Factors

Stress

The most common factor that drives anxiety disorders is excessive stress. The daily experience can put you under significant pressure. You may have worry about different things, including the state of your health, relationships or financial status.

These concerns could make you feel that things are going to get worse, thereby worsening or keeping up your anxiety. Stress may actually induce you into taking some actions that may aggravate the problem.

Substance use

One of the dangers of excessive stress is the potential to drive those affected into substance use or abuse. When you are under significant stress, there is the tendency that you may turn to alcohol or maybe illegal drug use.

Research has shown strong link between anxiety and substance use. The relationship seems to go both ways. People with abuse substances are more likely to experience severe anxiety symptoms. Also, those with anxiety disorders are significantly more likely to abuse alcohol or other drugs. Talk about a vicious cycle.

Certain medications and supplements

Illegal or controlled substance are not the only problems with anxiety, but also regular drugs your doctor may recommend to you. Anxious feeling could be a side effect of these.

Notable among the drugs that may contribute to anxiety disorders is caffeine. This stimulant encourages the kind of "fight or flight" response seen in anxiety. What this means is that symptoms may worsen rapidly with the use of this drug.

Another medication that may cause or worsen these mental illnesses is benzodiazepine. This drug, which is interestingly used to treat anxiety, may cause the problem to worsen if you stop taking it abruptly.

Apart from these two, there are several others that may promote anxiety disorders. They include cold medications and thyroid drugs.

Ingredients in supplements, including those for weight loss, may be problematic as well. For instance, guarana and green tea extracts may promote anxiety due to their high caffeine content.

Heredity

Like some other mental conditions, anxiety disorders may run in the family. The implication of this is that it may be correct to state that you may experience any of them if either of your parents or another close relative has any.

Your genes could make you more sensitive to situations in ways that other people are not. You may find yourself worrying a lot about things that other people seem to be less concerned about. The disorder makes your system to overreact to stimuli that carries little or no risk.

Medical conditions

Other medical issues can also fuel the development of anxiety disorders. Notable among this is heart problem. People with heart conditions often exhibit anxiety symptoms, including palpitations and shortness of breath. These symptoms can linger for longer than a year.

Issues affecting the endocrine system can promote these illnesses as well. They can lead to hyperactivity of the nervous system.

Among the other risk factors for anxiety disorders are:

- Poor economic status
- Being female
- Behavioral inhibition (shyness) in childhood
- Loss of a loved one
- Being divorced

How are Anxiety Disorders Diagnosed?

Diagnosis of these mental illnesses is not always an easy affair. The reason for this is that there are not really objective biomarkers to rely on. Doctors typically work with the evident symptoms.

For your anxiety to be suspected as a disorder, you must have been experiencing it for at least six months. It needs to be assessed as being excessive in relation to the stimuli and must have adverse effect on normal functioning.

Diagnosis often involves the use of any of different types of questionnaires.

Usually, your doctor will first make attempt to rule out other underlying medical conditions by running tests for them. Effects of drug use would also be evaluated. Your doctor may suggest you see a mental health professional, such as a psychiatrist or a psychologist, if he is not able to detect the physical cause of the problem.

A mental health specialist can work with you to design the best treatment plan for your anxiety disorder, if you are found to have it. Treatment usually involves the use of medications and/or psychotherapy, the so-called "talk therapy."

There are a number of other things you can also do on your own to promote rapid improvement.

S.E. Charles

CHAPTER 2 - TYPES, SIGNS AND SYMPTOMS OF ANXIETY DISORDERS

There are various types of anxiety disorders. While practically all have certain symptoms in common, they also have some distinctive symptoms that set them apart from others.

In this chapter, we discuss the different types – the most common ones, that is – of these mental illnesses. You will also learn about signs and symptoms that may be suggestive of each one.

Generalized Anxiety Disorder (GAD)

Characterized by excessive worry or fear that may carry on for months, GAD is a common type of anxiety disorders. It especially qualifies for the description of "irrational" in that there is no specific object or situation that induces it.

People who have generalized anxiety disorder worry about everything. They worry about their job, family, appointments and practically every other thing that demands their attention.

As you can see, the affected individuals worry about normal everyday matters. GAD has possibly set in when this trend continued for at least six months.

GAD patients exhibit several anxiety symptoms. Experts say you may suspect the disorder if you have at least three of the following symptoms:

- Fatigue
- Restlessness
- Irritability
- Muscle tension
- Sleep problems
- Concentration issues

The disorder can affect your decision-making ability, among other negative effects, as well.

Panic Disorder

As you may be able to guess from the name, this anxiety disorder contributes to panic attacks. It causes you to experience an intense feeling of fear or terror from time to time without any prior warning. The attacks can last from a few minutes to several hours.

Although the particular triggers are often unknown, panic attacks seen in this disorder may be the result of stress. They may also arise from random, irrational thoughts or general fear of the unknown. Exercise may also cause them.

The nature of possible attack triggers means that, with panic disorder, it is impossible to prevent all cases of an attack. In fact, fear of future episodes is enough to induce intense terror in a patient.

Distressing symptoms that you may observe with this condition include:

- Shaking or tremors
- Sweating
- Palpitations or pounding of the heart
- Chest pain
- Dizziness
- Shortness of breath
- Fear of losing control
- Choking
- Fear of dying

The symptoms that panic disorder may bring about could cause an affected person to think they are dying. They sometimes cause such individuals to quickly check in at a hospital as a result.

Often, panic disorder is present along with other forms of mental or anxiety disorders.

Social Anxiety Disorder (SAD)

An individual with SAD is usually afraid of being in a public gathering, especially being the point of attention. Such people have fears or worry about being opposed, humiliated or embarrassed in social settings. They generally don't feel comfortable about being the object of public scrutiny.

Again, it is not entirely odd for a person to feel a bit uncomfortable in these situations. The real concern is when it continues for six months or more.

Also known as social phobia, SAD causes affected individuals to avoid situations that make them feel uneasy, such as public speaking. Those affected endure such situations with great unease, if they must.

This mental illness often has a connection to perception of one's body image.

Signs and symptoms of social anxiety disorder include:

- Being afraid of what people might say or think about you
- Avoiding places where you may need to interact with others
- Trembling or sweating when in a social situation
- Feeling of being sick in the stomach
- Difficulty in making or keeping friends
- Being self-conscious

If care is not taken to address it, SAD can drive you to total social isolation. It is capable of making you feel uncomfortable whenever you find people around you.

Agoraphobia

This is a type of anxiety disorder in which the person having it is afraid of being in a situation where it may be hard or embarrassing to escape. It is also fear of being in a state where one might not have access to help to prevent panic symptoms.

There is a strong link between agoraphobia and panic disorder. The symptoms of the mental illness are often set off by fear of having a panic attack. A sufferer usually needs to be assured of an escape route being in view to keep calm.

A person with agoraphobia typically is afraid of being in a crowd, open spaces, enclosed spaces, or of using public transportation. They may also be anxious about waiting in line or leaving home alone.

When exposed to any of these triggers, the symptoms that may manifest are similar to those of panic disorders, including:

- Rapid heart beat
- Dizziness
- Excessive sweating
- Chest pain
- Fear of dying

A diagnosis is only possible when the fear experienced is intense, or rather excessive, and interferes with normal activities.

Specific Phobias

These are mental disorders that involve intense and persistent fear of a particular situation, object or activity that is usually harmless. Specific phobias represent the single, largest group of anxiety disorders. It is estimated that up to about 12 percent of the global population has them.

People with specific phobias are usually afraid of what could happen when exposed to the object of their fear. Common phobias include fear of flying, spiders, water transport, blood, and tunnels.

An encounter with the object of fear can result in symptoms that are, to an extent, similar to those from panic attacks. Among them are:

- Fast heart rate
- Trembling
- Shortness of breath

People with agoraphobia are commonly aware that their response to object of fear is excessive, but they are helpless to do anything about controlling it.

Separation Anxiety Disorder

This type of mental illness involves excessive fear of being separated from people or places one is closely connected to. While it is normal for anyone to feel a bit anxious about being separated from a loved one, the degree of this in the case of separation anxiety disorder is extreme.

This condition affects both children and adults. It is believed to be more common among adults but tends to be more severe in children.

Separation anxiety is a normal part of childhood development; the only concern is when it gets excessive. When separated for even just a short while, some children with this disorder may be in panic.

Possible symptoms include:

- Unwillingness to be away from object of affection
- Fear of losing a loved one to death
- Excessive and recurrent distress
- Frequent nightmares about separation

While physical symptoms of separation anxiety disorder typically develop in childhood, they can persist into adulthood.

Other Types of Anxiety Disorders

There are still other forms of anxiety disorders apart from the major ones mentioned. A consensus appears to be lacking as to whether these other types can truly be described as such.

Obsessive-compulsive Disorder (OCD)

The main characteristics of this disorder, as the name suggests, are obsessions and compulsions. The obsession part has to do with recurrent, undesirable thoughts or images, while compulsion refers to repetitive behaviors. These are usually not the effect of a physical condition or use of drugs.

The repetitive behaviors in OCD include frequent hand-washing, cleaning, checking or counting. They are usually performed in the hope that they could help deal with fearful thoughts. However, these only provide temporary relief.

The ICD-10 recognizes this as an anxiety disorder, but the DSM-5 no longer does.

Post-Traumatic Stress Disorder (PTSD)

Here is another mental illness that the DSM-5 no longer recognizes as an anxiety disorder, although some other sources do. PTSD is a condition that arises due to a traumatic or terrifying event of the past. Such events include bullying, rape, accidents, disasters, or combat.

Sleep disturbance is among the possible symptoms of this disorder. Others include flashbacks, anger, and hypervigilance.

Anxiety can have significant adverse effect on your health. It is important to seek the opinion of your doctor if you suspect any of these disorders. Experiencing some of the symptoms we mentioned above for six months or more may be considered a red flag.

CHAPTER 3 - TREATMENT OPTIONS FOR ANXIETY

Anxiety disorders are more common than many people might realize. For instance, according to the National Institutes of Health, about 18 percent of people 18 years or older in the United States have at least one type of anxiety in an average year.

The associated anxiety or worry can get in the way of important things in a person's life. It can certainly make you come across as an odd person around other people.

Thankfully, however, there are diverse options available for treating the disorders. The specific approach for tackling each one depends on the cause and extent of the problem, among other factors.

Broadly speaking, doctors mostly rely on psychotherapy or behavioral therapy and medications. The choice is often a combination of treatments rather than to use one form by itself.

Medications

Doctors may recommend a number of drugs for fighting your anxiety disorder. These, by no means, offer a cure, but rather provide relief from the associated symptoms.

Medications are more likely to be employed in the earlier stage of treatment. But there are cases where they are used when patients fail to improve from psychotherapy alone.

Here are some of the drugs that you may be prescribed.

Anti-anxiety Medications

These are also known as anxiolytics. Popular examples are benzodiazepines, which are common first-line interventions for generalized anxiety disorder.

Anti-anxiety medications help in reducing anxiety symptoms and checking panic attacks. They do this by correcting neurotransmitter imbalance that may be causing these effects.

Antidepressants

Drugs that are used for fighting depression can also prove useful for anxiety disorders. The most commonly prescribed are selective serotonin reuptake inhibitors (SSRIs), which are also first-line treatments for generalized anxiety disorder.

They help to improve the brain chemistry, thereby controlling anxiety symptoms. Examples include sertraline (Zoloft) and fluoxetine (Prozac).

You may need to use antidepressants for many weeks before noticing any improvement. They also carry risk of side effects such as headaches and sleep problems.

Beta-blockers

Also referred to as beta-adrenergic blocking agents, these medications are used for a variety of medical issues, including hypertension. They help, mainly, to address physical symptoms in the case of anxiety disorders.

Beta blockers inhibit norepinephrine and epinephrine, or adrenaline, from attaching to beta receptors on nerves. This makes them useful for addressing rapid heart rate, trembling, and chest pain that may accompany an anxiety disorder.

You may need to use some of these medications for a year or longer. But doing that can also increase risk of side effects.

Psychotherapy

It is less likely to experience rapid improvement in symptoms of anxiety disorders by relying on just medications. It is for this reason that their use is often combined with psychotherapy or behavioral therapy. There is actually evidence that the latter might be the more effective approach for treatment.

Anxiety therapies don't merely aim to control symptoms. They also often try to tackle the root cause of the problems, teaching affected individuals' skills to deal with them. This probably explains why they are often the preferred choices.

Psychotherapy or behavioral therapy, also referred to as talk therapy, is just a form of counseling. It involves speaking with a mental health specialist, such as a psychiatrist or psychologist. The treatment is ideally tailored to the needs and conditions of individual patients.

There are two main types of psychotherapy that are used for treatment of anxiety disorders. They are cognitive behavioral therapy (CBT) and exposure therapy.

Cognitive Behavioral Therapy

CBT has been proven to be very effective for dealing with these mental illnesses. It is regularly used as a first-line intervention for patients. Interestingly, you don't have to be physically present at your mental health specialist's office for it to work.

This therapy has as its target helping patients to recognize the cause of their anxiety and to alter their thinking patterns. In essence, it assists in conditioning their response to situations or things that cause them to be afraid.

CBT helps to identify negative patterns and distortions while also helping to change how you react or respond to them.

As the name suggests, "cognitive" has to do with knowledge of how your thoughts may lead to anxiety. The "behavior" aspect pertains to how you react to these thoughts or in certain situations.

Through this therapy, you can learn skills that you can use to combat your anxiety disorder. You get to learn how to think, behave and react in situations that may induce anxiety.

For instance, with CBT, you can learn to stay calm when exposed to a situation that normally causes you panic attacks. It can also help you realize that these episodes are not heart attacks.

Cognitive behavioral therapy has been found to be effective for different types of anxiety disorders. Among these are generalized anxiety disorder, social anxiety disorder, and specific phobias.

Some patients are reported to experience improvement with this therapy in as little as about three months from commencement.

Exposure Therapy

This treatment aims to help you get better by exposing you to the same situations that make you to feel anxious. You might think that is a crazy thing to do. But it is not exactly how you probably think it is. This is why specialists are ideally in charge of these therapies.

Exposure therapy is based on the idea that you can never fully overcome your anxiety if you are wont to avoiding objects or situations that cause you to become afraid. It therefore aims to help you gain better control by exposing you to these same things.

To make this process easier, it is carried out in a controlled manner. It can be very traumatizing if you dare to face your fears without caution.

The therapy begins with systematic desensitization. This is a gradual approach to fighting your fear. You start at a level that is only a little frightening and you build on from there. This teaches you how to use relaxation and breathing techniques to deal with a phobia.

Your therapist will likely develop a step-by-step approach that you can use to gradually get over situations that cause you to be anxious. These steps are specific, and you need to spend enough time in each to fully overcome the associated distress.

This approach helps to gradually desensitize patients until the triggers become controllable or are entirely dealt with.

However, exposure therapy doesn't appear to be as effective as cognitive behavioral therapy.

Other Treatment Options

There are also other means of treating anxiety disorders apart from psychotherapy and use of medications. Most of these are mainly concerned with changes in your lifestyle choices.

Stress management

It is well known that stress is a major trigger for anxiety disorders. Doctors, therefore, usually advise that patients take steps to keep it from getting too overwhelming.

For instance, it helps to be more organized and have to-do lists to avoid pressure from deadlines. Also, set time limits for work or study.

Exercise

Experts think that patients can also benefit from physical exercise. This can promote the release of certain "feel good" chemicals in the brain. It can also be beneficial for improving your body image.

Relaxation Techniques

You can get help from methods or practices that help you relax as well. These can help to alleviate anxiety symptoms or keep them from developing.

Examples of these techniques are breathing exercises, acupuncture, and meditation.

Lifestyle changes that can also be beneficial for improving symptoms include getting better sleep, putting an end to smoking, and cutting down on your caffeine intake.

An effective treatment program will often combine several of the different available options. How fast your symptoms improve will depend on the severity of your anxiety disorder, among other factors.

CHAPTER 4- TIPS FOR MANAGING YOUR ANXIETY

Anxiety disorders are often misunderstood – many people think that you can simply overcome the symptoms by willpower. While it's important to seek professional treatment, it's also important to adapt your lifestyle.

Here are some tips that have been proven to be helpful for managing Anxiety.

Accept yourself

It is not uncommon to find people with anxiety disorders looking down on themselves... so to speak. This is not helpful. It can actually just make things worse.

There is nothing wrong in accepting that you have an anxiety problem. The problem is when you now think that it makes you appear like an odd person. As we noted earlier, this feeling is perfectly normal – everyone experiences them.

Even when it has transitioned to the stage of a disorder, realize that you are not alone. Millions of people face the same challenge across the United States.

So, don't put yourself down for feeling anxious. Experts say that it helps to admit to yourself when feeling anxious and accept that it's normal and will only last a short while.

Confront your fear

Accepting that you have anxiety is great, However, you need to go beyond just accepting that you are having an anxiety problem. You can think of that as the first step.

Mental health professionals say that it is crucial to face up to those situations that cause you to be anxious. Trying to avoid them is one of THE major factors that causes the problem to get worse.

Dare to find out that particular thing that causes you to be afraid while other people seem to be less concerned. They may actually not be real threats at all. But you will never find out if all you do all the time is run away.

Avoidance allows space for your anxiety to grow wings. You can fight this and get better by trying to find out the worst that can happen by confronting your fears. Find out whether your concerns are indeed justified.

Researchers at the Anxiety and Depression Research Center at the University of California found that individuals with anxiety issues were better able to cope after they exposed themselves to known triggers.

Do things that challenge you... Be adventurous... Don't always try to avoid risk and uncertainty.... as doing so is actually believed capable of intensifying anxiety rather than alleviating it.

Realize that nobody is perfect

Some cases of anxiety disorders have a connection to

self-perception – the manner in which you consider yourself, especially in relation to others. This is bad.

This is not something that is often said…. But…While it is a good thing to always seek to be better, you should be careful not to set too high standards for yourself. That is capable of putting you under considerable stress, causing an increase in anxiety.

It is helpful to realize that nobody has it all. While other people might appear to be doing better in a certain way, be aware that they also have their weaknesses. Their flaws might be your own strong points… the difference is… they are probably not as worried.

Have more realistic expectations to live your life by.

Put your worries on hold

One thing with anxiety is that troubling thoughts don't usually give a notice before popping up. You could be in the middle of something interesting and they come up, somewhat extinguishing the excitement.

You should learn to put those disturbing thoughts on hold for the meantime when they come up. Ricks Warren, a clinical psychiatry associate professor at the University of Michigan, describes this to The Huffington Post as a "worry postponement or scheduling" technique.

Say, for instance, you are in the middle of a favorite activity and you start getting anxious about something you need to do afterwards. You can simply say to yourself: "This is not the right time for these thoughts, I will think about the task later at a proper time." You then try to shift your attention back to the present.

You might find that when you start attending to that task later on it might not be as daunting as you probably thought it to be. But if it is, you can get some help.

Learn to calm yourself

It will also be helpful to learn about ways to stay calm when in anxious situations. Normally, you would rest your body when you feel physically strained. Your mind also needs help to cool down when subject to anxiety.

Do things that help to you to relax. There are different relaxation techniques that could prove helpful. Breathing techniques can help you stay calm. Meditation and yoga are among means for relaxing your mind.

Often, things that help to relax your body also assist in calming your anxiety.

Less-intensive, but exciting activities, such as a stroll, music listening, or book reading, can also be calming.

Exercise

Exercise offers one of the best ways for dealing with anxiety. There is significant and convincing evidence of anxiety symptoms improving when you work out.

It can produce the same effects as drugs for mental health disorders, such as selective serotonin reuptake inhibitors (SSRIs). It helps to boost and balance neurotransmitters in your brain to make you feel good.

Exercise presents a very useful distraction from situations that may be inducing your anxiety. It can help to reduce muscle tension and stress. It improves your sleep and energy levels, making you livelier.

And exercise doesn't always have to be something that you do in a gym. Practically anything that causes you to move and exert yourself qualifies. Dancing, gardening, swimming, biking and walking are also forms of exercise.

Enlist a loved one

Recruiting a caring, listening loved one to help enables you to express your anxiety. Holding it up inside can have serious negative effects on you, both physically and psychologically.

It is important to make some changes to be able to battle this mental condition more effectively. This may be a tough thing to do entirely on your own. The reason is that these changes may involve doing things you normally dread doing.

The support of family or friends can be helpful in changing things you do and how you do them. Having a loved one around may make it easier to attempt things you'd ordinarily not have done because of anxiety. You just need to be certain they understand the problem and how they can help.

Be organized

You can get help in managing your anxiety by becoming better organized. Prepare to-do lists and break seemingly daunting tasks into smaller steps. Try to plan everything you need to do.

Not being organized has a way of increasing your anxiety, say, when you have a deadline to beat. This reflects as procrastination and indecision.

Your anxiety reduces when you break each project or goal into smaller bits and attend to each part at set times.

Get quality sleep

Anxiety and sleep are not complementary; there is a sort of inverse relationship between the two. When you are highly anxious, it is highly likely that it will have negative effect on your sleep. This further worsens the problem. Yet, you actually need quality bedtime to be able to improve symptoms.

Therefore, it's up to you to make more conscious efforts to ensure you get better sleep. A good first-step is to organize your life. Make your bedroom to be in a state that encourages sleep. Certain foods can also help, just as putting an end to the screen-staring well before you go to bed.

These tips should help you to better manage your anxiety, but if you should ever feel that tackling your anxiety problems on your own is too daunting and overwhelming, it would be sensible to seek professional help.

CHAPTER 5 – HOW EXERCISE AFFECTS YOUR ANXIETY

Virtually all of us are aware of the difference exercise can make in the health of a person. The benefits you get from it are not only physical in nature, but also extend to mental health. This is why it is considered an integral part of effective treatment program for anxiety.

Your body and mind are not exactly independent. The thing that affects one will most likely impact the other. There is a strong link between the level of your physical activity and state of your mental health.

There is considerable evidence that exercise can be helpful to people with anxiety and other mental health issues. It has been found to be as effective as some medications for treating these disorders.

Benefits of Exercise for People with Anxiety

Many studies have highlighted the physical benefits of exercise - how it helps to prevent medical conditions and diseases. It is little wonder then that doctors usually recommend it to those with real interest in promoting good health.

Studies have also revealed different benefits that exercise offers for boosting mental health. It has been known to help:

- Boost your mood
- Improve alertness
- Enhance focus and concentration
- Fight tension and stress
- Increase energy levels
- Reduce mental fatigue
- Increase motivation

Exercise also helps you get better quality sleep. This can be beneficial for reducing stress and dealing with anxiety.

It is for this reason that therapists often try to evaluate the activity level of patients when it comes to treatment. This is a way of ascertaining whether lack of exercise could be a possible issue.

How Does Exercise Help?

While there's plenty of agreement on the benefits, researchers do not fully understand the exact means by which exercise helps to relieve anxiety. They believe this could be the result of the effect it produces on the brain's chemicals.

Stress is a major factor in the occurrence of anxiety, as you may be aware. It affects your brain, with the impact being felt by the entire body. Exercise helps to battle this problem.

Researchers believe that when you engage in physical activity, the brain produces chemicals that help you deal with stress. Perhaps, the most notable of these are endorphins.

These substances help to relief pain and promote feeling of relaxation or euphoria. This makes it easier to get quality sleep and so reduce stress-induced anxiety.

Exercise also helps to boost brain-derived neurotrophic factor (BDNF) levels. This protein facilitates the repair of cells in the brain that stress damages.

Some also say physical activity increases endocannabinoid levels. It boosts body temperature, an effect that interestingly helps to calm you down.

What's more? Exercise has a way of helping to improve your body image. This can boost your confidence and self-esteem, making it easier to function better in social situations.

Best Exercises for Anxiety

For some people, what comes to mind is a daunting and uninteresting activity at the mention of the term "exercise." But that's not exactly true. You can think of it as anything that makes you more physically active.

Exercises that can help the most for controlling anxiety aren't necessarily exhausting activities such as marathon running or weightlifting. The following are among the ones that are considered most beneficial for those who suffer from anxiety.

Yoga

this ancient practice is known to be very helpful for dealing with anxiety disorders. Its movements, breathing methods, and meditation offer a great means for promoting calmness. Once you can manage to adjust to the poses, you are on your way to getting better.

in a study conducted in the aftermath of the 2004 Andaman tsunami, studies found that yoga promoted significant reduction in select markers of anxiety in survivors. These markers were heart rate, breath, and skin resistance.

Pilates

You can also combine this exercise with yoga to improve your results. Regular Pilates can help to strengthen your core. It also improve your posture, with this capable of making you feel and look more confident.

What's more? The exercise helps you to release tension, relieve stress, and fight insomnia. It may also improve your mental clarity and creativity.

Running

This is arguably one of the best exercises you can do to experience great health. It enhances both physical and psychological wellness. It helps to fight mental disorders, including anxiety, through effects on neurotransmitters, including serotonin and norepinephrine, in the brain.

Running can make it easier for you to get quality,

restful sleep. This is beneficial for reducing stress and enhancing memory, among other benefits. Experts have also observed that exercise seems to have similar effects as meditation on the brain.

Zumba

There are some people who describe this dance-based exercise program as the best for people with anxiety issues. The routine, which emerged in the 1990s, involves moving to Latin beats, such as salsa and flamenco. It is most likely because this feels more like fun than exercise is the reason many people love it so much.

This is unlike your regular aerobic exercise. It integrates a spirit of community, which can be very helpful to anxious people.

Zumba helps to improve anxiety as a result of mental focus that is involved, according to a study in Games for Health Journal. This combines with the fact that it is very exciting.

Exercise and Panic Attacks

Panic attacks are among the symptoms of anxiety disorders. One would expect that exercise should help to deal with them. However, it has been detected that you can exacerbate these attacks when you hit the gym.

When you exercise, it is normal for your breathing and heart rate to increase. Adrenaline also increases.

Sadly, these changes are similar to those seen in panic attacks. A person with panic disorder may take them as signs of an attack, leading to a downward spiral. This can worsen the anxiety problem.

Just as exercise increases "feel good" chemicals in the brain, it is also capable of raising the levels of cortisol. People with panic disorder are especially sensitive to this stress hormone. Their body responds to it in a manner that even encourages further production.

Strangely, it has been found that exercise promotes lower cortisol levels in the long run. Which means people having panic attacks can still benefit from being physically active.

You just need to find a way for your body to adapt to exercise in the short term. One of the ways to achieve this is by going slowly. Rather than exerting yourself for like 20-30 straight minutes at a time, you may start with a minute or two. You could then increase duration gradually as your body adapts.

It may help as well to consider doing your exercises in a place you find comfortable. This is especially beneficial to those who feel very anxious being in a public setting.

How Much Exercise Will Do?

The amount of time you need to exercise to enjoy good mental health depends on your fitness and level of intensity.

The common recommendation for adults when it involves moderate activity is about 120 to 150 minutes per week. You don't have to spend that much time at a go. You can break it into 20 or 30 minutes a day.

For more intense workouts, the amount of time is usually lower.

The most important thing is to ensure you get moving. Being physically active in any way and for whatever length of time is better than doing nothing at all.

Experts even say you can get relief from your anxiety with just roughly 5 minutes of aerobic exercise.

CHAPTER 6 – HELPING A FRIEND OR FAMILY MEMBER WITH ANXIETY

Do you have a friend or family member that currently suffers from an anxiety disorder? It can be rather confusing and intimidating understanding how they feel. You may find it saddening seeing what they experience.

Chances are that you don't know how you can help them to get better, even though you wish you could. It is also possible that you are already "helping" in your own way but they don't seem to be improving.

Here are some suggestions that you will find useful when it comes to helping a friend or family member with anxiety:

Let them know they can always talk to you

It can be very helpful to your loved one when he or she knows they have someone they can rely on. Let them know that you are available to discuss whatever thing may be causing them to feel anxious.

You should strive to instill confidence in them that you won't judge them for feeling the way they do. The confidence that they have a listening and understanding person to depend on can make great difference in their recovery.

Get informed

One of the first-steps you want to take to be truly helpful is to get educated about anxiety. Without this, you are not likely to be of much help to your friend or family member. You can't really give what you don't have.

Make an effort to learn practically everything worth knowing about the particular anxiety disorder and its symptoms. There are more than enough resources on or offline to fall back on.

Find out what helps with the disorder. Best treatments may differ between the diverse types of these mental illnesses.

By getting more informed about anxiety, you are less likely to become frustrated with your loved one. It will reduce the chances of making insensitive statements like "just snap out of it, will ya!"

Let them know that you don't find them odd

There is a sort of stigma that people with anxiety problems carry with them. They tend to feel fearful of being embarrassed by symptoms in front of others. They worry that other people may think of them as been weird or inferior.

It helps to assure your friend or family member with

such issues that you don't consider them abnormal. Try to let them know that anxiety is not an indication that they are worse than other people.

It may help to let them know that it is not entirely abnormal to feel the way they do in certain situations. What is important is that they can learn skills to cope in such situations.

Remain calm

What happens in an anxiety episode is that your fear, which may be rational or irrational, sets off multiple changes in your body. The symptoms that are observed are simply manifestations of these changes. When your loved one sees these symptoms, they may become more fearful.

Therefore, they will benefit greatly if they can learn to stay calm. This might not look as easy as it sounds, but it is possible. Staying calm helps to disrupt the stress response.

You can make it easier for the friend or family member by staying calm yourself. When they notice your serenity, they may find that reassuring for calming their nerves.

Find out how you can be of help

It is possible that your loved one already has an idea of what they can do to control anxiety. They have probably gone through useful resources at some point in the past.

So, your friend or family member may know already what they can do to calm down but are helpless. You make it easier for them to know the situation is well under control by showing your readiness to help.

For instance, you may be helpful to someone with social anxiety disorder when they request that you make yourself available for support in social situations.

Don't encourage avoidance

It's very likely that the help your friend or family member might want from you is to help them avoid situations they fear. You might think you are helping them by agreeing to such requests. But sadly, you are not.

Psychiatrists reveal that avoiding avoidance is among the proven means of successfully breaking free from anxiety. Running away from anxious situations, on the other hand, reinforces it. You need to help them face up to that "scary" task or situation.

Take the case of an assignment at a workplace, the more they postpone it, the more they worry about how they are going to complete it.

You can help them to break the overall task or goal into pieces or steps. Taking one step at a time can prove useful for avoiding avoidance.

You can also encourage them to put the skills they learn from therapies, such as cognitive behavioral therapy, into use.

Don't put too much pressure on them

The flipside of helping a loved one to break free of avoidance is pushing them too hard. Do not expose them to anxiety inducing situations they may find overwhelming.

This means you should encourage your friend or family member to face their fears, but exercise caution if they express great fear or already start to show sign of distress. You can instead look to do this gradually.

It will be counterproductive trying to force someone

into doing things they fear when they are not adequately prepared for such. This will most likely worsen the problem.

Give a listening ear to your loved one in trying to help them overcome avoidance. Make the process easier by taking one step at a time. For instance, first get someone with fear of dogs comfortable about being around them before asking him or her to consider playing with them.

Encourage your loved one to get professional help

It might prove too much for you to successfully help a friend or family member overcome anxiety. If you do come to this realization, try to encourage him or her to seek professional help. There is often a limit to how far self-help can go.

Ask if you can help them get an appointment with a doctor. In some disorder cases, patients may be afraid of leaving home. You can suggest having a doctor come by in such a situation.

Help them find a good therapist. Psychotherapy methods, such as CBT, can be of immense help in learning to cope with anxious feelings.

And when they start getting professional help, try to find out what new things they are learning. You can use such information when it comes to assisting and supporting them.

Find out if there is something they wish their therapist can improve on or something they don't find helpful. It is not uncommon for people with anxiety disorders to have reservation about discussing such with a therapist.

Help to get your loved one to open up about these with their mental health professional for improvement or *possible adoption of alternative strategies.*

Celebrate whatever progress they make in the course of treatment, however little. Let them feel how important the small progress can add up to significant improvement over time.

Take care of yourself

It can be pretty demanding watching out for a loved one with anxiety. If you are not careful, it can take a considerable toll on you.

You want to be sure not to take on more than you can handle. Consider sharing support with another friend or family member. This will enable you to be in a good enough state to continue in the role.

It will be to your advantage, and indirectly that of your friend or family member with anxiety issues, to have someone you trust whom you can share your own feelings with. This will be beneficial especially to your mental health.

CHAPTER 7 – ALTERNATIVE TREATMENTS AND REMEDIES FOR ANXIETY

While there are conventional treatments for anxiety disorders, including drugs, some people are interested in alternative treatments instead. One of the reasons for this is the mistrust some people have for pharmaceutical companies. This, combined with the inefficiency of some medications and the side effects they produce.

Aside from that, more and more experts seem to agree that alternative treatments and remedies for anxiety can help some people get faster improvement.

Here are some of the options available that you may want to try out.

Time Management Skills

It is common knowledge that having many things to attend to at the same time is one of the factors that stoke anxiety. Having a clear plan of action will be helpful for keeping you from feeling anxious when confronted by many commitments.

It helps to improve your time management skills. Develop a step-by-step approach for attending to tasks before you. Each task or commitment should have its set time – a scheduler will help here. This can also helpful for avoiding multitasking, which can contribute to anxiety.

Exercise

As discussed in previous lessons, A great way to take your mind off your worries, even if only for a moment, is by getting active. Exercise has this way of boosting your moods with regard to how it fine-tunes your brain chemistry.

There is significant evidence that it helps with different medical disorders, including anxiety and depression. Exercises that increase your heart rate for about 30 minutes can be valuable for relieving stress and anxiety.

It was observed in a 2015 review of studies that exercise may be an effective treatment for anxious persons.

Breathing Techniques

Being in control of how you breathe can help you manage anxiety more effectively. It is not uncommon to lose control of how you breathe when feeling anxious. You will benefit from techniques that enable you to stay in control.

One of the things you may want to try to do when starting to feel anxious is to be still. You may find a chair to sit in with your back straight.

Next, try to breathe in deeply through your nose with

your diaphragm raised. This helps to improve circulating oxygen in your body, making you feel less tense and anxious. Then slowly breathe out through your mouth.

You may repeat the process all over until you feel calm.

Yoga

More people are now aware of the benefits of yoga, this system of breathing, motion and meditation. There are also studies proving its potential effectiveness. Yoga is among the top 10 alternative treatment for disorders, including anxiety, according to the Anxiety and Depression Association of America.

The practice helps to relax your mind. It lowers stress and helps you to be less anxious about life.

In a recent research at a mental health hospital in New Hampshire, it was shown that yoga can be beneficial for anxiety. Subjects became less anxious and experienced lower levels of tension, anger, and fatigue, among other negative feelings. These effects came after only one class.

Meditation

Meditation offers a great way of clearing the mind. It helps to bring about a desirable state of consciousness or frame of mind through breathing, control of thoughts, focus, prayer or mantras. You ideally do this in a quiet, calm setting.

With meditation, you get help in relaxing both your body and mind. It may help you realize the source of your anxiety and helps with the process of overcoming.
It doesn't take the causes of your stress and anxiety away. The practice only conditions how you respond to

them.

Massage

Tense muscles are common when people are having anxiety. This usually happens involuntarily as they freeze and/or clench their jaw when anxious.

Massage can help to relieve tight muscles. The therapy is useful for improving the flow of blood to certain parts of the body. This can help you to feel relaxed, discharging stress and anxiety.

Aromatherapy

This alternative treatment refers to use of essential oils and miscellaneous aromatic plant compounds for promoting good health outcomes. Some people call it essential oil therapy.

Aromatherapy basically involves smelling soothing oils or other compounds. This helps to relieve stress and improve mental functions. The aromatic oils and compounds that are used promote feeling of relaxation.

Examples of essential oils that are commonly used include chamomile, lemon, peppermint, and lavender.

Results from a 2012 study showed that this therapy may help to slow heart rate. It also helped to address sleep problems. Researchers used lavender in the study.

Acupuncture

This ancient Chinese practice is about the use of needles to promote good health. Among the problems that it has been found beneficial for are anxiety and depression.

In acupuncture, a practitioner sticks fine needles into the skin at given points on your body. The aim is to correct the flow of energy, or Qi, to facilitate wellness.

Disruption of this flow is thought responsible for diseases.

The technique provides pain relief by activating certain chemicals in the brain. It is thought capable of relieving anxiety symptoms. There are reports of some people getting over anxiety with acupuncture.

Cranial Electro-Stimulation

Cranial electro-stimulation (CES), also known as cranial electrotherapy stimulation, is a relatively new treatment approved by the U.S. Food and Drug Administration for treatment of anxiety and some other conditions. It is a non-invasive means of stimulating the brain.

CES involves the use of a small device to deliver small, pulsed electric current to the brain. This helps to stimulate the organ and the cranium, thereby possibly helping to lower anxiety.

Although some studies have been done on it, cranial electro-stimulation isn't very popular for treatment of anxiety.

Supplements

Supplements are also among the alternative options available for treatment of anxiety. While there is a bit of debate on their usefulness, there are reports of people improving with them.

Dietary supplements and herbs that may potentially be useful include:

L-Theanine – This is an amino acid that you will get from natural sources, such as green tea and black tea. It is included in some supplements. L-Theanine is believed to help fight stress and reduce anxiety.

Omega-3 – There is promising evidence that this may be helpful to people with anxiety. It was found in a 2011 study at Ohio State University that students who took Omega-3 supplement showed lower anxiety, compared to those who used a placebo.

Valerian – This supplement comes from the root of a perennial plant called Valeriana officinalis. It helps to combat sleep issues and anxiety. Although popular, there is no consensus in research yet as to its ability to make you feel less anxious.

St. John's Wort – Botanically known as Hypericum perforatum, this plant is increasingly becoming a popular alternative treatment for anxiety and depression. But research seems to back its use for the latter condition more.

Kava kava – The root of this plant is a popular beverage in the Pacific Islands. Some people in the West are now using it to fight anxiety. Researchers have found some similarities between its effects on brain wave activity and those of diazepam (better known as Valium).

In one study, it was observed that the anxiety levels of the subjects got better after taking Kava kava for a week.

It is important to note, however, that some of these supplements come with potential side effects. For example, valerian may cause upset stomach and headaches. Kava kava could bring about serious side effects including liver damage.

Final thoughts

It's ultimately best to first check with your doctor if you are considering an alternative treatment. This way, you will be able to reduce the risk of negative effects.

You can enhance the efficiency of your treatment plan for anxiety by including complementary and alternative therapies. It may not be enough to rely on them alone.

Please Leave a Review

Finally, if you enjoyed this book, please take the time to share your thoughts and post a review. It'd be greatly appreciated!

That review and feedback will help me improve the content in my books – and make each and every one more relevant and helpful to you.

Thank you again and good luck!

S.E. Charles